rithee, good folk, listen to me!
Her most noble Majesty, Queen Elizabeth I, who recently
departed this world, had no children. Thus she was the last of our great
Tudor monarchs. Before Her Majesty died, she bid me write down
tales, both tragical and comical, from Tudor times for your pleasure.

I was in my tenth year when I came to Queen Elizabeth's court,
and I soon became her favorite scribe. I hope that I have done Her
Majesty justice in writing these tales, and that they will help me
leave my mark on the realm. So, I entreat you, read on. I will try
to entertain you right royally!

Arthur Inkblott
May 1603

PS — Beneath the Tudor tales you will find scenes from the lives of
Tudor common folk. At the last count there were some four million of
these peasants in all of England and Wales.

PPS — Pray allow me to introduce my ferret, Smudge. He lives
in the margins of this book and has much to say. I beseech you, be
careful, for he has often nipped a passing finger!

For Thom, with love.

Off with his head!

Just a joke!

First U.S. edition 2016

Library of Congress Catalog Card Number pending
ISBN 978-0-7636-8122-7

16 17 18 19 20 21 APS 10 9 8 7 6 5 4 3 2 1

Printed in Humen, Dongguan, China

This book was typeset in Truesdell, Yuletide, and Perry Gothic.
The illustrations were done in watercolor, ink, and gouache.

Candlewick Press
99 Dover Street
Somerville, Massachusetts 02144

visit us at www.candlewick.com

THE TUDORS

·Kings·
Queens·Scribes
and
·Ferrets!·

WRITTEN AND ILLUSTRATED BY

MARCIA WILLIAMS

HELPED BY ARTHUR INKBLOTT

CANDLEWICK PRESS

The Wars of the Roses

For thirty years, a great civil war raged across England. I was not alive to witness it, but it is still spoken of with awe. It was caused by two noble families, known as houses, fighting for the right to rule. One was the House of York, whose symbol was a white rose, and the other the House of Lancaster, whose symbol was a red rose, so the battles were known as the Wars of the Roses. I tremble to imagine how long these wars might have raged if Henry Tudor, a noble Welshman from the House of Lancaster, had not arrived in England.

· MOST PEOPLE LIVED IN THE COUNTRY OR IN SMALL MARKET TOWNS ·

The Battle of Bosworth Field

Prepare to die, imposter!

'Tis said Richard III murdered his own nephews!

His reign was not a happy one.

He was the last English king to die in battle.

Who'd want to be a royal?!

Royal blood is tops!

ᚻenry Tudor led his troops against the unpopular King Richard III, of the House of York. They met at Bosworth Field in Leicestershire, where they fought the last great battle of the Wars of the Roses on August 22, 1485. Although King Richard bravely defended his crown, many of his soldiers and their noble commanders defected to Henry's side — and so King Richard was slain! His crown fell from his helmet and rolled beneath a bush. From there it was retrieved and placed on Henry's head, and the reign of the Tudors began — or so the minstrels sing!

Apples for sale.

Give us a farthing, Sire.

· LIFE WAS NOT EASY · JOBS WERE FEW, AND MANY STRUGGLED TO MAKE ENDS MEET ·

Who Was Henry Tudor?

No more Richard III!

Henry thought God had chosen him!

SECRET: Henry wasn't very Welsh.

TOP SECRET: Henry wasn't very royal.

You can tell by the taste of his blood!

When Henry was sure that all in Leicestershire knew Richard had been killed, he traveled on to London.

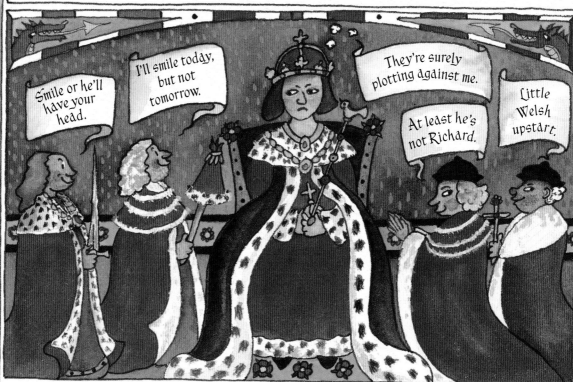

There, on October 30, 1485, a chilly autumn day, Henry was officially crowned Henry VII. He was just twenty-eight years old. As a child he had lived in France with his uncle Jasper, so he was unknown to most English people. But this did not deter our young Tudor, for like his many descendants, he had a fine brain and buckets full of ambition!

· COUNTRY FOLK WORKED FOR RICH LANDOWNERS · THEY RENTED SMALL PLOTS OF LAND

Henry was born at Pembroke Castle, Wales, in January 1457.

His father, Edmund Tudor, died before his birth.

His mother, Margaret Beaufort, was thirteen when he was born!

Henry's father had no claim to the throne.

Henry's mother could trace her ancestry back to Edward III.

At least twelve people had more right to the throne than Henry.

Including his poor young mother!

This made Henry feel very insecure.

He had won the crown, but how would he keep it?

Most girls married at age fourteen.

Ferrets marry at eight months!

Traitors risked torture . . .

or even execution!

Torture sours the blood.

TO GROW THEIR OWN CROPS AND GRAZED THEIR FEW ANIMALS ON COMMON LAND ·

Henry VII Rewrites History!

Tudors believed God was all-powerful.

Even a king had to obey God.

Henry's claim to the throne was fishy. . . .

He was wearing another's crown!

Henry won the Battle of Bosworth Field, so Parliament believed God had chosen him as king. But a goodly number of nobles thought he had no right to the throne. Henry had to act fast to keep them from raising armies against him, so he declared that his reign had started the day before the battle. This meant everyone who had supported Richard III was a traitor — and Henry executed many of them: chip, chop, aaagh! He threw the rest into the Tower of London. If they tried to escape, he executed them, too!

· IF EXTRA FOOD WAS HARVESTED, WOMEN SOLD IT AT MARKET · FEW PEASANTS

A Royal Wedding

Hurrah for King Henry VII!

This will bring peace.

Verily, she is most fair.

Hurrah for them both!

A great way of defeating the Yorkists!

If Henry was to hold on to his crown, he needed to do more than execute a few unfriendly nobles. So he married Elizabeth of York, even though he had never met her before the wedding, to unite his House of Lancaster with her House of York. On the day of the wedding, London was thronged with cheering crowds. Everyone hoped that the marriage would bring peace to England.

Henry cleverly joined his red rose of Lancaster with the white rose of York to create the Tudor rose. He plastered his new rose everywhere he could think of, including buildings, coins, flags, and banners. Now even his most illiterate subjects would see that it was their great Tudor monarch, Henry VII, who had united the houses and brought an end to the Wars of the Roses!

Tudor monarchs had great brains . . .

but did they have great morals?

Zzzzzzzzz . . .

He'll DEFINITELY lose his head!

No lice today.

Money

Henry never imposed a ferret tax.

Maybe he didn't fancy being the first fingerless king!

Tudor monarchs liked absolute power.

Henry liked getting his own way!

I will banish you if you keep fighting!

Henry VII won his crown in battle, but he was no warrior.

Is there not even one groat?

Not one, Sire.

Wars were expensive, and Henry had inherited a very poor realm.

No new gowns, no wine, cheap beer...

To save money he cut palace spending, including the queen's.

Poor nobles are more loyal.

PRITHEE, PAY YOUR TAXES HERE

PAY UP OR DIE!

I can't afford a sword, let alone an uprising.

Then, to refill England's empty purses, he imposed heavy taxes — especially on wealthy nobles. This increased the country's wealth, but it did not help Henry's popularity.

Pay £10,000 to guarantee your loyalty and I'll say no more about the poisoned wine.

Henry also created a system of bonds so that displeasing him became very costly.

Guilty! A large fine or death?

I'll take the fine.

He made great use of the Star Chamber, a court where even the most powerful lords could be tried and fined!

Henry's full title: Henry, by the Grace of God, King of England and of France and Lord of Ireland

I'm flipping exhausted!

Stop moaning, woman, I've been up since cockcrow.

We all work hard.

Spare us some beer.

That I will, friend.

· PEASANT WOMEN WORKED VERY HARD · THEY CLEANED AND COOKED AND LOOKED

Power

Henry used some of his newly acquired wealth to increase his own security. He was the first English monarch to have his own bodyguards: the Yeomen of the Guard.

Henry made it illegal for nobles to raise private armies.

He also created a network of spies across England and Europe.

Anyone reported to be plotting against him was executed.

He did reward loyal subjects, but only if it didn't cost too much!

Henry ruled for nearly twenty-four years, but he was never able to stop worrying about money or plots to steal his crown!

Henry liked large presents.

Lots of large presents . . .

land, money or castles!

Fleas prefer a dog to a human.

Depends which is juiciest!

AFTER THE CHILDREN · THEY MADE BUTTER, CHEESE, BEER, AND THE FAMILY CLOTHES ·

Christopher Columbus

Early Tudor maps weren't accurate.

America wasn't on them.

Columbus navigated by the sun and the stars.

Only two of his three ships made it home.

COLUMBUS'S FIRST VOYAGE
NORTH AMERICA
ENGLAND
ATLANTIC OCEAN
SPAIN

Land ahoy!

During Henry VII's reign, all trade between Europe and Asia happened either over land or via the recently discovered African route, by sailing around the Cape of Good Hope. But Italian navigator Christopher Columbus decided to sail west to find a new, safer route to Asia, which was rich in treasure. In 1492, supported by Queen Isabella of Spain, Columbus set off. After many weeks he sighted land. Columbus thought he had reached East Asia, and he returned to Spain a hero! He died never knowing that he hadn't found a shortcut to Asia . . . he had landed on America!

In fourteen hundred and ninety-two, Columbus sailed the ocean blue.

Go yonder and call the midwife.

I go!

I go, too, for this is women's work.

18 HOURS LATER

Lord, 'tis but a puny thing.

· WOMEN OFTEN DIED IN CHILDBIRTH OR FROM AN INFECTION AFTER THE BABY WAS BORN ·

Columbus had asked Henry VII to fund the voyage, but Henry thought it too risky; he was more interested in the arts and new ideas coming from Europe than in exploration. He encouraged French and Italian scholars and artists to visit England. He also supported England's first printer, William Caxton, causing many scribes to fear for their jobs! But when Henry heard that Columbus had returned with exotic treasures, including turkeys, parrots, and gold, he changed his mind about sea voyages! So in 1497 he sent his own explorer, John Cabot, off to seek treasure in North America.

· A WOMAN'S AVERAGE LIFE EXPECTANCY WAS ONLY THIRTY-FIVE YEARS ·

Henry VII's Family

A son was vital to a king.

A spare son was a bonus.

Girls didn't usually inherit the crown.

Women were supposed to serve and obey!

Arthur Tudor	Margaret Tudor	Henry Tudor	Mary Tudor

Henry VII had married Elizabeth to save his crown, but she was kind and clever, and he grew to love her. They had eight children, but only four survived infancy.

"A" is for apple.

Elizabeth taught her children to read and write.

"T" is for Tudors.

Henry helped the tutors teach his sons history.

I am the best!

He made sure they had the best tutors available.

That's my boy — we are the greats!

Henry favored his eldest son, Arthur — heir to the crown and his hope for a Tudor dynasty!

All the more time to enjoy my sports!

His younger son, Henry, was just a spare. He was not expected to take on royal duties.

The king was in his counting house, counting out his money. The queen was in the parlor, eating bread and honey.

One night's pee!

That's nothing, watch this!

Poop!

I was going to drink that!

· OPEN SEWERS RAN THROUGH THE STREETS, AND SEWAGE CONTAMINATED RIVERS ·

Margaret & James IV of Scotland

Mary & Louis XII of France

Arthur & Catherine of Aragon

Henry VII arranged marriages for his children to help keep the peace with neighboring countries.

I may not be so spare after all!

In 1502, five months after marrying, Arthur died of a fever.

We will have another child.

Henry VII was devastated, but he was comforted by Elizabeth.

You're all I have left.

In 1503, Elizabeth gave birth to a daughter. She and the baby died.

Can't I go outside?

No. Help me make money!

Henry retired to his private apartment at Richmond Palace to mourn. He stayed there for most of his final years. Henry VII had avoided foreign conflict and brought peace and prosperity to England — not bad for an unknown Welshman. The Tudor monarchy was off to a strong start, and Arthur's younger brother Henry was ready and waiting to carry on the Tudor dynasty!

Ferrets get to choose their mates!

Infant death was very common.

Henry never married again.

The fleas will now sing a Tudor song!

The maid was in the garden, hanging out the clothes, when down came a blackbird and pecked off her nose!

Come, buy my fresh water!

Water'll kill ye!

Verily, mine's purer.

Buy our freshly brewed beer.

Oink, I love a good dung heap!

And one for baby.

• THERE WAS NO RUNNING WATER, AND LITTLE WAS UNDERSTOOD ABOUT HYGIENE OR GERMS •

Babies were wrapped tightly in cloth.

This was called swaddling.

Henry composed music.

He also wrote poetry.

Lullay, baw, baw, my bairn, sleep softly now. . . .

When Henry was born on June 28, 1491, at Greenwich Palace, nobody expected him to become king. Yet he had his own servants from birth — even rockers to rock his cradle. He was nicknamed Hal, and he was a beautiful baby who was often dressed in smocks and petticoats.

TOP MARKS

Latin
English
French
Italian
Spanish
Greek

Am I not a star, Mama?

Remember, Henry, it is all a gift from God.

TOP MARKS

Math
Science
History
Geography
Music
Astronomy

Even as a toddler, Hal was lively, charming, and slightly spoiled. He was very close to his mother, Elizabeth. She encouraged him in everything he did, and he pleased her by excelling at all his lessons. He was also fantastic at sports, including tennis, archery, dancing, hunting, riding, and jousting.

A line from Prince Hal's pen: "The time of youth is to be spent, But vice in it should be forfent." (*Forfent* means *forbidden!*)

I've got the sweating sickness.

Bloodletting!

I've got a fever.

Leeches!

I've got smallpox.

Herbs!

I've got gout.

Worm paste!

• MEDICINES WERE MOSTLY MADE OF HERBS AND INSECTS • COMMONERS COULDN'T

The king was always well guarded at night.

Hal was only eleven when his brother Arthur died and he became heir to the throne. It was a bit of a shock! Suddenly, he was expected to give up dangerous sports and spend more time at court.

A dog or ferret on your bed protects you from fleas!

Young Hal always said his prayers. . . .

Hal's father told him to get engaged to Arthur's widow, Catherine of Aragon. She was seventeen — six years older than Hal. Yet she was bright, funny, and enjoyed sports. Better still, she had a pet monkey and loved to dance, so the betrothed couple got on very merrily.

They say hell's flames will get you if you don't!

We never bite priests. We don't want to go to hell!

AFFORD DOCTORS • DOCTORS USUALLY HAD NO IDEA WHAT CAUSED DISEASE! •

Henry VIII – The Headstrong

Hal was a spark of life after his dad.

Hal loved his new wife to bits!

She was so charming and kind . . .

she could almost have been a ferret!

Spanish blood is very tasty!

We'll call him Bluff King Hal.

He's right royal.

Verily, he's 6' 4" tall.

A kingly stature.

In April 1509, just before Hal's eighteenth birthday, his father, Henry VII, died. Hal and Catherine were married shortly afterward. Then, on June 24, with great pomp and ceremony, Hal was crowned King Henry VIII and Catherine was crowned as his queen. Their coronation was a day of joy, for this handsome young prince brought new hope to his kingdom. Two days of jousting and feasting followed.

'Tis an auspicious day!

You're right, there.

There's fairy magic about.

Aye, bread magically vanishes!

That's not magic, that's thieving!

· A CORONATION WAS A CHANCE FOR COMMONERS TO CELEBRATE ·

• HENRY AND CATHERINE'S CORONATION TOOK PLACE ON MIDSUMMER DAY •

Palaces and Potties

Hal loved clothes and jewels.

Hal loved mattresses, too.

Lots of them!

It took ten men to make his bed and search it for assassins.

It took millions of fleas to fill it!

Not bad for a butcher's son!

Wolsey, who had started life as a mere butcher's son, loved fine palaces and buying expensive things.

Thy ring is beauteous!

I thought so, too.

Unfortunately for Wolsey, Hal also loved fine palaces and expensive things.

Just one more castle . . . **Yes, my lord!**

Hal had inherited seven palaces and fourteen castles, but enough was never enough for him.

No rush, but move out by tomorrow!

When Wolsey rebuilt Hampton Court Palace, Hal liked it so much, he took it!

My ladies are not yet packed. **Then they are late!**

When Hal got bored, or a palace began to smell, he would just move to another one. His courtiers, his many hundreds of servants, and all his furniture traveled with him.

We got the handsomest king in Europe.

He's a true royal!

But does he care about us poor folk?

Poverty is God's punishment for our sins. Or for Hal's sins . . .

· COMMON FOLK LOVED HENRY VIII EVEN THOUGH THEIR LIVES DID NOT GET ANY EASIER ·

As there were no drains and waste wasn't cleared very often, palaces quickly became smelly. At Hampton Court there was a room of lavatories called the Great House of Easement that could sit twenty-eight courtiers at a time — what a stench! Hal had his own velvet-covered toilet and a Groom of the Stool to wipe his bum. He often suffered from constipation — methinks he ate too much meat. In one year his court ate 8,200 sheep, 2,330 deer, 1,870 pigs, 1,240 oxen, 760 calves, 53 wild boar, and zero ferrets!

J'adore French food!

Mmm!

Je déteste jousting!

King Henry was very vain.

King Francis was also vain!

Fleas have no time for vanity.

When Hal came to the throne, he wanted to prove what a fine warrior he was, so he stirred up old quarrels with France and Scotland. His general, the Earl of Surrey, defeated the Scots at Flodden Field, killing King James IV of Scotland. Meanwhile, Hal won a battle against the French. Then, in 1520, Francis I, the French king, invited Hal to Calais to talk peace and play games of skill. Francis wanted Hal to be his ally as he was surrounded by the realms of the Holy Roman Emperor, Charles V: Spain, Holland, and Germany.

Hide, or they'll commandeer ye.

'Ere you, out!

You must fight the French.

· MANY COMMONERS WERE RECRUITED INTO THE ARMY · THOUSANDS LOST THEIR LIVES

PILLORY, THE STOCKS, TORTURE, HANGING, AND EVEN BURNING AT THE STAKE •

Henry's Six Wives

Henry began to behave most unkindly.

A ferret never casts off his wife!

Anne was clever and feisty.

A French swordsman beheaded her.

Divorced, beheaded . . .

CATHERINE of ARAGON

Thou hast grown old and wrinkled.

Thou hast grown old and crabby.

ℌal was married to Catherine for twenty-four mostly happy years. He jousted as "Sir Loyal Heart" and laid trophies at her feet. She bore Hal six children, but they all died except for Mary, born in 1516. Hal divorced Catherine when his wish for a son became overwhelming. After the divorce, she left court and never saw her daughter again. She died in 1536, still calling herself Queen Catherine.

ANNE BOLEYN

Thy neck is so tempting!

My neck is yet young, my king.

ℌal's marriage to Anne in 1533 divided England. Many people stayed loyal to Catherine and the Church of Rome. Anne had a daughter, Elizabeth, in September 1533. Then she miscarried a baby boy. Hal was furious and wanted to divorce her. His minister, Thomas Cromwell, advised against a second divorce, so Anne was accused of courting other men. This was treason, so Anne was beheaded.

JANE
SEYMOUR

My dearest and best wife.

Henry was 45 when he married Jane.

He was balding and growing portly!

Swans symbolize love and loyalty.

Jane was a lady-in-waiting to Anne. She refused Hal's advances while he was married, but in 1536, eleven days after Anne's execution, she married him. Jane blamed Anne for Hal's break with the Pope and his mistreatment of English Catholics. She wanted to influence him for the better. On October 12, 1537, their son Edward was born. After twenty-eight years and three marriages, Hal had a male heir at last! Sadly, twelve days later, Jane died. Hal was heartbroken. He was buried beside Jane when he died.

died . . .

Henry gave Anne a large pension.

She remained in England.

Kate was young and flirty . . .

a little *too* young and flirty.

divorced, beheaded . . .

ANNE of CLEVES

In May 1539, Hal ordered Cromwell to find him another wife. Finally, Hal picked Anne of Cleves, the sister of a German duke. When Anne arrived in England, she did not resemble the flattering portrait that Cromwell had shown Hal, but it was too late to stop the wedding. Hal couldn't upset the German duke by beheading Anne, so he divorced her and beheaded Cromwell!

CATHERINE HOWARD

Hal married Catherine in 1540, on the day Cromwell was beheaded. She was nineteen, and Hal was forty-nine. Thomas Cranmer, head of Hal's new church, was not keen on Catherine, as she was a Catholic. He accused her of being unfaithful to the king. This was treason, so Catherine was beheaded after only eighteen months of marriage.

KATHERINE PARR

I have my fool to make me laugh and you to rub my toes.

Verily!

Henry's fool was named Will Somers.

Nobody else dared to tease Henry like Will did.

Henry believed worms could cure him.

There's no fool like an old fool.

When Hal and Katherine Parr got married in 1543, he was fifty-two and not a great catch! He was so fat he could hardly walk and had to be carried on a special chair. His lungs were bad, he was constipated, he had gout, leg ulcers, and bouts of fever, and he was very grouchy. Katherine was a kind, obedient wife and a devout believer in the Church of England. She was loved by Hal's children, Mary, Elizabeth, and Edward, and she brought them to live together at court for the first time. Katherine remained married to Hal until he died.

survived!

The Death of Bluff King Hal

Hal signed execution warrants on his deathbed.

Hal's split with the Catholic Church led to a conflict....

Protestants fought Catholics.

Catholics fought Protestants!

Fleas fought for blood!

That's my boy.

In early January 1547, Hal felt too ill to spend time with his queen or even his beloved fool. He retired to bed, and on January 28, he died at age fifty-five. Hal left England poorer and in a state of religious turmoil: the new Protestants who wanted worship to be simpler were fighting with the Catholics. Thousands of people had been executed during Hal's reign, and thousands of others had died in pointless wars. What had happened to Bluff King Hal whose coronation had brought hope and joy? Some suggest he had damaged his brain in a jousting accident. Or perhaps he had just become a cruel tyrant. It may never be known. Yet in his "great matter" Hal had succeeded — he had left a son, Edward, to carry on the Tudor dynasty!

Who will feed us now?

Hal did it for the best.

We'll starve.

I'll die.

The monks fed and clothed us.

They taught me Latin.

I had a job!

• HENRY CLOSED THE CATHOLIC MONASTERIES, SO THE POOR COULD NO LONGER TURN TO

The Short Reign of Edward VI

Hal's son was only nine when he became King Edward VI, so his uncle, the Duke of Somerset, became Lord Protector and governed for him.

Edward and Somerset were both Protestants and upset the Catholics with new laws that banned many of their religious rites.

There was also growing discontent amongst the peasants as landowners stopped them from renting plots or grazing their flocks on common land.

Somerset did little to restore harmony, and in 1550 he was replaced by another Protestant, the Duke of Northumberland.

Three years later, Edward became ill, and Northumberland began to worry about his safety if Mary, Edward's Catholic sister, became queen. He persuaded Edward to name Henry VIII's Protestant grand-niece, Lady Jane Grey, as his heir. In July 1553, Edward died and Northumberland declared Jane queen!

Queen Mary 1

I've only got one religion.

FOOD!

I fight over it a lot.

But I always win!

You can guess our religion!

QUEEN JANE
July 10–19, 1553

I smell ferret!

I have suffered enough humiliation in my life without that upstart!

Lady Jane Grey was fifteen when she was proclaimed queen. She had little claim to the throne and even Protestants believed Mary was the rightful queen. After only nine days, Queen Jane was overthrown, and eventually both she and Northumberland were executed. Mary became queen, but her subjects were in for a shock! Mary had hated her father for heartlessly divorcing her mother and declaring her illegitimate. She had turned to her religion for comfort and now felt it her sacred duty to restore the Roman Catholic faith and purge England of Protestants.

KEEP OUT!

But they're my turnips.

Billy's hungry.

KEEP OFF!

But that's our grazing land.

· WHEN LANDLORDS THREW COMMONERS OFF THEIR FIELDS AND ENCLOSED COMMON

"Catholics rule now!"

Mary scrapped Edward's religious laws and revived Catholic services.

"Run for your life!"

Protestants began to fear for their lives, and hundreds fled the country.

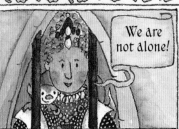

"We are not alone!"

For a time, Mary even imprisoned her Protestant sister, Elizabeth.

"I will terrify my people into being Catholics."

Protestants suffered terrible persecution. Many were tortured or burned at the stake.

"A message from the Pope." "My dream come true!"

To Mary's joy, England was received back into the Roman Catholic Church.

"I can't wait to return to Spain."

Mary married Prince Philip of Spain. He was a committed Catholic like she was.

"What were my sister's last words?"

"Keep on persecuting Protestants!"

Mary longed for children and suffered two phantom pregnancies. In late February 1558, she retired to her room believing she would soon give birth — but there was no baby. Mary never recovered and died in November. As she had no heir, the crown passed to her half sister and my most perfect patron, Elizabeth.

Elizabeth was a brave prisoner.

Around 300 Protestants died at the stake.

Luckily, Elizabeth wasn't one of them.

God bless Good Queen Bess!

"More Tudor blood!"

"Can you spare a halfpenny? We're starving and homeless."

"Begging and vagrancy are crimes. Into the pillory!"

NO ENTRY!

Queen Elizabeth I

God be praised for Elizabeth.

Henry's third child to rule.

Henry made all that fuss about a male heir!

He just needed a girl with a ferret's brain!

My people are my children.

England is my husband.

On January 15, 1559, Elizabeth Tudor was crowned Queen of England. She was twenty-five years old, and Parliament was keen for her to marry. Elizabeth politely refused.

Majesty, my quill is weary.

Well, your queen is not!

ZZZZZZ

Like her father in his youth, Elizabeth was clever and beautiful. She loved riding, poetry, music, and dancing. Yet she never neglected her duty and often worked late into the night.

She loves him.

She loves him not.

She loves him ...maybe not!

Good Queen Bess, as we liked to call her, also enjoyed flirting with handsome courtiers and even servants! The Tudor court was again alive with feasts, merriment, and intrigue.

Clench poop!

Puh!

Dolt!

Carpet knight!

Cod's head!

Gore belly!

Not that it was all fun, for Bess had a wicked temper! I myself saw her slap, spit, and throw shoes at those who displeased her!

Here's a song about Elizabeth: "Ride a cockhorse to Banbury Cross to see a fine lady upon a white horse. . . ."

A queen?!

Verily, 'tis a laugh!

Might as well have a child monarch.

Or the local idiot!

Her dad'll turn in his grave.

· MANY COMMON FOLK DID NOT BELIEVE THAT A WOMAN COULD RULE ·

Live here, good Queen, live here, You are amongst your friends. Their comfort comes when you approach, And when you part, it ends.

Majesty, I have built you your own tower, private garden, boating lake, and hunting lodge.

She looks like a goddess.

Her skin is as white as a lily!

WARNING: The plague often hit London in the summer.

It was safer to leave the city when the weather was hot!

Moving about also helped avoid smelly toilets.

Me and Arthur are keen on that!

Unlike her father, Bess had not inherited great wealth. She liked beautiful clothes and jewels, but sometimes she was forced to sell these to raise cash. In the summer, Bess saved money and met with her people by going on "progresses" around the country. Bess and her court would stay with nobles along the way. They were expected to entertain Her Majesty lavishly — even if it meant bankrupting themselves!

Rings on her fingers and bells on her toes, she shall have music wherever she goes."

'Ave you seen her?

She's pretty.

And clever.

And charming.

Long live Good Queen Bess.

· BUT ELIZABETH SOON WON HER SUBJECTS OVER WITH HER DEDICATION AND EASY CHARM ·

Mary, Queen of Scots

There were many plots against Queen Bess.

Many traitors were beheaded.

Mary wore a red petticoat for her execution.

Her dog hid underneath her petticoat.

There is a lot to be said for a good dog!

You no-good Catholic!

You no-good Protestant!

Good Queen Bess had inherited a country split by religious discord.

One's subjects must be moderate.

Bess was a Protestant, but although she was quick–tempered, she hated extremists.

We will allow moderate Catholics.

She wanted both moderate Catholics and Protestants to be accepted and live in harmony.

A Protestant can't be queen!

Many people hated that idea. They wanted a Catholic monarch to rule the country.

I am the most perfect of all Catholics.

Bess's cousin Mary, Queen of Scots, was a keen Catholic contender for the throne.

Will you protect me, dear cousin?

Mary fled to England after her husband died. Many people believed she'd had him murdered.

Throw away the key!

Bess knew Mary was after her crown, so she locked her up for the next nineteen years.

Shh! This letter will be the death of the queen!

Unfortunately, this did not stop Mary from plotting against our Good Queen Bess.

Farewell, world!

Finally, Bess lost patience with Mary. In 1587, she signed Mary's death warrant.

We are charmed to meet you.

Please, heal me.

All them jewels! She's a picture.

Heal my puppy.

The Spanish Armada

The death of Mary, Queen of Scots, did not end the Catholic threat. King Philip II of Spain also wanted England to be a Catholic country again. In 1588, he invaded England with a fleet of ships called the Armada. Our sailors loaded empty ships with gunpowder, set them on fire, and then drove them toward the Armada. The Spanish sailors tried to turn their huge ships around, but in their hurry they bumped into one another. Then a great storm came and most of the Spanish ships sank!

Philip had deserted Queen Mary I.

Now he wanted her sister's crown!

Luckily, Bess had spies all over Europe.

Plus a few clever admirals!

A sailor's blood comes ready-salted!

I kissed her hand once.

Liar!

She's an angel.

Our guardian angel.

I love her.

Hurrah for Good Queen Bess!

THEM AND TOUCH THE SICK, AS THEY BELIEVED SHE COULD HEAL THEM ·

Sir Francis Drake

1540–1596

B oth before and after the Armada, Spanish ships sailed to and from South and Central America and returned to Spain loaded with gold, silver, and other treasure — a perfect target for pirates! Our dear queen, having no liking for the Spanish, turned a blind eye to English pirates who relieved them of their hoards. A favorite buccaneer was Sir Francis Drake. He was knighted by our gracious queen after becoming the first Englishman to sail around the world. Drake also helped lead the attack against the Spanish Armada, but they say he paused to finish his game of bowls first!

Sir Walter Raleigh

Wat and I eat Spaniards on potatoes for breakfast!

We do, Dad.

It was tough being a sailor . . .

False love, desire, and beauty frail, adieu! Dead is the root whence all these fancies grew.

1552–1618

Majesty, you are my only Tudor rose!

eating nothing but salt meat, peas, and bread . . .

Verily, thou dost know how to treat a queen!

Majesty, I blush.

Creep!

and trying to sail heavy ships.

Many sailors died at sea.

Sir Walter Raleigh was another of Bess's favorite adventurers. Little mattered more to a Tudor noble than valor, gallantry, and honor, and Raleigh had ink pots full of these! He was a fearless soldier, a fine poet, and was extremely handsome. He led many expeditions to America and introduced potatoes and tobacco to England. It is said he once threw his velvet cloak over a puddle so that Her Majesty would not dirty her dainty shoes. He did fall out of favor, though, when he secretly married one of Bess's ladies-in-waiting. He was locked up in the Tower of London until the queen forgave him!

Flea explorers traveled by rat!

No land, ahoy!

We'll starve.

I've lost all my teeth and hair!

Shall we mutiny?

Think of the rewards if we'd returned with treasure!

· THIS MEANT MORE JOBS BOTH ON LAND AND AT SEA, SO THERE WAS LESS POVERTY ·

William Shakespeare

That very time I saw, but thou couldst not,
Flying between the cold moon and the earth,
Cupid all arm'd: a certain aim he took
At a fair vestal throned by the west,
And loos'd his love-shaft smartly from his bow
As it should pierce a hundred thousand hearts;
But I might see young Cupid's fiery shaft
Quench'd in the chaste beams of the watery moon,
And the imperial votaress passed on,
In maiden meditation, fancy-free.
⌐ A Midsummer Night's Dream, Act II, Scene 1

Bravo, Will!

Eek!

Bess banned religious plays to stop unrest.

Secular plays were much more fun!

I fancy I would make a marvelous actor!

Our Good Queen Bess encouraged not only trade and exploration but also the arts, which are far closer to the heart of a scribe. Bess's court was a haven for writers, poets, scholars, musicians, and dramatists. Jubilations! Our dear Majesty was a generous patron, especially to one Mr. William Shakespeare, an actor and playwright of great repute. I have even had the honor of transcribing one of his plays! Londoners still flock to the new theaters to watch them. Listen out for the theater's trumpeter if you want to know when the play is about to start!

Theaters were alive with fleas!

'Ere, that toff called me a stinkard!

Well, you are, mate.

Do you like Will or Mr. Greene best?

Shut up and listen to the play!

I'd rather watch the bear-baiting!

Will is an upstart crow!

Eeeeeek!

'Ere, Will, you're meant to be speaking to me - Titania!

The king doth keep his revels here tonight.

The Globe Theater opened in 1599.

Female parts were played by men or boys.

Some theaters were used for bear-baiting, too!

Many of Shakespeare's plays were also performed at court, for as our dear queen grew older she was less inclined to venture into public places. I suspect that many of Shakespeare's plays were written to keep his queen and patron sweet of temper and generous of mood. I myself was privileged to watch *A Midsummer Night's Dream*, which was written for a special court performance. Our Bess blushed with pleasure when the fairy king, Oberon, honored her with some most flattering lines.

We used to perform in a flea circus.

Buy my fine apples!

Shh!

Shh!

Hot pies for sale!

Ooh!

I can't hear the words.

I know every line by heart. . . . Ah, Juliet . . .

Ah, Romeo!

POORER COMMON FOLK WERE KNOWN, STOOD THROUGHOUT THE SHOW ·

The End of the Tudor Dynasty

Poor Bess hated growing old.

She hid her gray hair under a red wig.

She hid her wrinkles under white makeup.

She only bathed every three months!

Fleas hate baths!

We are most unhappy.

In March 1603, several of Good Queen Bess's closest friends and valued advisors died.

We are at home here.

Queen Bess felt melancholy and retired to Richmond Palace, her favorite home.

We are not ourself.

Her strong spirit seemed crushed and she began to grow weak, but she refused to go to bed.

Majesty, rest yourself.

For three days and nights she stood upright in her room — perhaps hoping to avoid death.

Who will follow you?
Our cousin James of Scotland.

She neither ate nor slept, and her worried ladies-in-waiting stood ready to stop her from falling.

At last, Good Queen Bess sank down onto the cushions that had been laid at her feet.

She grew so weak that she was unable to object when her servants carried her to bed.

Musicians came to soothe her with soft music until she fell into a deep sleep.

The Tudor dynasty has ended.

Her breathing grew shallow and then stopped. Our dear queen had slipped from this world.

I hereby proclaim that our good queen . . .

Verily, a sad moment.

Baa!

It'll be a male monarch next.

• THE DEATH OF ELIZABETH SHOCKED HER SUBJECTS • MOST HAD KNOWN NO OTHER MONARCH

As Elizabeth had no children, she appointed a Protestant, James VI of Scotland from the House of Stuart, as the next monarch. The great Tudor dynasty had finally ended. There were over a thousand mourners in her funeral procession, including my good self, and thousands more lined the route. On top of the coffin lay an effigy of Queen Elizabeth dressed in her finest clothes. It was so lifelike that all who saw it gasped in wonder. Queen Elizabeth was buried in Westminster Abbey next to her half sister, Mary, who had once imprisoned her in the Tower of London.

Bess's dad would have been proud.

But Bess left no Tudor heir!

So it was out with the Tudors . . .

and in with the Stuarts!

Henry would have turned in his grave!

Men can't rule!

My dad does!

It'll be that Scottish king, James VI.

He'll be James I of England.

A male monarch. It'll never work!

AND FEARED THAT A KING MIGHT NOT RULE AS WELL AS THEIR GOOD QUEEN BESS! •